ROARING RIDES

MUSCLE CARS

TRACY NELSON MAURER

Rourke

Publishing LLC
Vero Beach, Florida 32964

www.rourkepublishing.com

Project Assistance:
Ed Newman, AMSOIL INC.

Also, the author extends appreciation to Mike Maurer, Alan Maurer, Frank Westman, Christopher Edling, Classic Corvettes and Collectibles, and Kendall and Lois M. Nelson.

Photo Credits: Title, 5, 6, 7, 12, 15, 19, 20, 21, 23, 30, 31, 32, 38 © John A. Schrils, Classic Corvettes
p. 8, 9, 11, 16, 17, 25, 28, 34, 36, 43, 44 © K-8 Images
p. 26 © Darren England - Allsport
p. 35, 40, 41 © Josh Gin (No Neck)

Title page: The Chevrolet Nova was one of the most popular muscle cars.

Editor: Frank Sloan

Cover design: Jay Foster

Page design: Nicola Stratford

Notice: The publisher recognizes that some words, model names, and designations mentioned herein are the property of the trademark holder. We use them for identification purposes only. This is not an official publication.

Library of Congress Cataloging-in-Publication Data

Maurer, Tracy, 1965-
    Muscle cars / Tracy Nelson Maurer.
        p. cm. -- (Roaring rides)
Summary: Discusses the history and current popularity of stylish, high-performance cars built beginning in the 1960s to appeal to young drivers, as well as how they have been adapted to keep up with emissions standards.
Includes bibliographical references and index.
  ISBN 1-58952-750-X (hardcover)
  1. Muscle cars--Juvenile literature. [1. Muscle cars. 2. Automobiles.] I. Title. II. Series: Maurer, Tracy, 1965-   Roaring rides.
  TL147.M36 2003
  629.222--dc21

                                    2003010020

Ppk 1-58952-926-X

Printed in the USA

w/w

MUSCLE
TABLE OF CONTENTS

CHAPTER ONE

Rock-and-Roll Cars

In the early 1960s, American carmakers realized young drivers did not want to putter around in their parents' stodgy **sedans**. Speed, power, and style mattered to the rock-and-roll crowd. Soon, two-door **coupes** with big, ready-to-race engines swept the country. Rock bands like the famous Beach Boys even sang about the fast and sleek cars.

The first Shelby Cobra appeared in 1962. It looked racy, much like this car, and sparked a new era for the car world.

Instead of plush comfort, muscle car interiors focused on speed and handling.

RULING THE ROAD

Songs about fast cars sounded nice. But most of the new high-performance cars rolling out of Detroit, Michigan, factories in the 1960s and early 1970s weren't meant to be nice. They were meant to rule the road.

Ford's Mustang hit the streets in 1964 and delivered record sales. The popular Mustang featured a long hood and short tail-end. People called them pony cars.

The Ford Mustang, such as this 1967 model, was one of the most popular muscle cars of the decade.

Many muscle cars also featured a shortened wheelbase—the distance between the front tires and the rear tires—such as the Chevrolet Camaro, Pontiac Firebird, and Plymouth Barracuda. They were called pony cars, too.

More than their shape, the smallish pony cars had huge horsepower. Their big engines growled with heart-pounding strength. Eventually, the powerful coupes earned the nickname "muscle car."

Powerful engines tuned for speed gave "muscle cars" their nickname.

The Plymouth Barracuda looked fast from headlights to tailpipes.

THREE GENERATIONS (SO FAR)

Muscle cars reigned from 1963 to 1973. Called the classic muscle cars, the first generation of powerful coupes set many speed records.

Two more generations of muscle cars followed the original heydays. Neither group re-captured the raw power and free spirit of the first muscle cars. Still, all muscle cars attract fans for one reason or another.

The first generation of muscle cars from 1963 to 1973 focused on speed and style.

The second generation of muscle cars from 1974 to 1987 lacked the spark of the originals. Still, who would turn down a 1982 Corvette?

The muscle car revived after 1988. Safer and friendlier to the environment, the stylish new models could bury a speedometer again.

The gasoline shortage and lower speed limits in the 1970s dented muscle car sales. Still affordable to buy, gas-guzzling muscle cars were very expensive to run.

ROAD BUMPS OF THE 1970S

Many disappointed car buyers from 1974 to 1987 claimed that second-generation muscle cars lacked power and speed. The vehicles looked tamer than the first generation, too. However, these muscle cars ran circles around some other cars of their day—the AMC Pacer, the Chevrolet Chevette, and the wanna-be Ford Pinto, for example.

Don't blame the carmakers for causing the wimpy years (although some of their models had grown stale by 1971). Many things happened in the 1970s to weaken the appeal of muscle cars.

In 1973, the Organization of the Petroleum Exporting Countries (OPEC) began an oil embargo that sent gasoline prices skyrocketing. Unfortunately, the big engines in muscle cars guzzled a lot of gas. Keeping the gas tank full became very costly.

Responding to the gas shortage in 1974, Congress encouraged states to adopt (and enforce!) a speed limit of 55 miles (88.5 km) per hour. Soon, the muscle car national anthem became the Sammy Hagar rock song, "I Can't Drive 55!"

AIR POLLUTION SOLUTIONS

Another blow to muscle cars came in 1975 with the Clean Air Act. This law required manufacturers to build cars that released only small amounts of **emissions**, or pollution, from the engines' exhausts.

Carmakers put **catalytic converters** on engines to reduce emissions. For muscle cars, this tool suffocated the engine's power. Catalytic converters required unleaded gasoline, too. Unleaded gasoline delivers less zip than leaded gasoline, like Kool-Aid without sugar!

Safety issues also hurt muscle cars along the way. Most drivers lacked the skill to handle high-performance vehicles. Car insurance rates climbed. Sales for muscle cars slipped even more. Without buyers, carmakers dropped muscle cars from production… at least, for a while.

REVVED AGAIN

By 1988, engineers figured out how to make muscle cars go fast again, even with emission controls. Designers also gave the third-generation muscle cars some of the original flair. Congress allowed states to set higher speed limits without funding penalties. No longer an all-American machine, several **imports** revved up the muscle car scene, too.

Rectangular side markers appeared in 1969 on the Plymouth GTX, also known as the "gentleman's super car."

ROARING FACT

The Beach Boys sang about a Dodge in the song "Little Old Lady from Pasadena" and the band sang about a Chevy in "My 409." All the major car manufacturers produced at least one high-performance car back then. Today, every fan of muscle cars has one clear favorite.

CHAPTER TWO

Sleek Style

All muscle cars look fast even when they're parked. Sleek body designs in the 1960s helped the cars gain speed and loyal fans. Dealers offered buyers more options than ever. For example, from 1965 to 1968, Mustang buyers could order a hardtop, **convertible**, or fastback coupe.

JUST FOR LOOKS

Stylists created exciting new finishing touches to give the cars a brute look. Again, buyers could pick and choose from lots of options. Bold colors, stripes, and graphic emblems separated these cars from Grandpa's Sunday-go-to-church land barge.

Even a basic Mustang convertible like this one looked fast.

Hood scoops, racing stripes, and other doo-dads gave muscle cars extra style.

Some of the stylish "bells and whistles" served no purpose. They just looked good. Fake hood **louvers**, fake column vents, and chrome doo-dads like sidewinder exhaust pipes and shiny ball-topped shifting levers tempted car buyers.

Chrome sidewinder exhaust pipes added more to the vehicle's look than to its performance.

PROVEN ADD-ONS

Of course, some of the stylish options could prove they worked. Air scoops in the hood looked menacing while forcing air into the **carburetor**. True, if a car's engine takes in more air to mix with the gas, then it can put out more power. So air scoops worked—if the car actually raced or hit top speeds on the open road. Everyday drivers really didn't benefit from air scoops.

The air scoop on the hood of this 1969 Mustang Mach-1 pulls in extra air at high speeds.

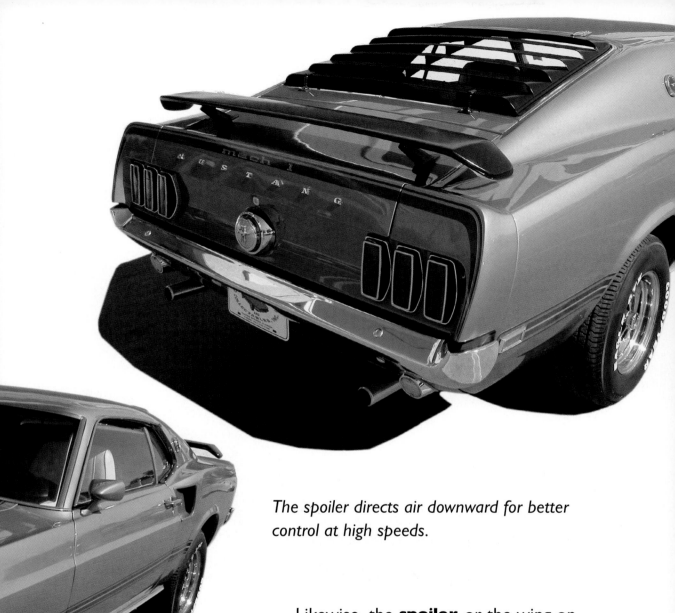

The spoiler directs air downward for better control at high speeds.

Likewise, the **spoiler**, or the wing on the trunk, directed air flowing over the car downward. This pressure helped the driver keep the car on the road—at very high speeds. Still, car buyers loved the sassy look of spoilers. They still do. Spoilers even appear on mini-vans today. Go figure.

Chevrolet offered its Camaro with many packages of exterior, interior, and engine options, such as Super Sport (SS), Rally Sport (RS), and Z-28. A buyer would custom-order a vehicle like he was ordering dinner in a fine restaurant. *"I'll take a '69 Camaro with the Z-28 package. Oh, and could you please make it a Rally Sport, too, please?"* For most drivers, muscle cars ran just as well without the options. But looks mattered as much as speed.

In 1969, Chevrolet made 12 different engine sizes for its popular Camaro.

ENGINEERING IMPROVEMENTS

Even now, the first model year for a car usually showcases its style. In the following years, the engineers take over and fine-tune the performance. The engineers often strip off the silly extras and replace them with ways to improve handling, speed, or comfort.

Fortunately for first-generation muscle cars, engineers spent most of their time tinkering with the engines.

Road Rockets

A first-generation muscle car with a **stock** engine cruised at serious speeds. Most cars were geared for **acceleration**, not cruising. People loved to see how fast the cars could go from 0 to 60.

The rare 427 V-8 in a 1969 RS/SS Camaro could blast off from 0 to 60 in 5.4 seconds or less. That was almost 2 seconds slower than a 1966 Cobra.

THE GTO MISSILE

Muscle cars generally didn't handle corners well, but they could fly on the straightaways. Drag races ruled. Two cars would race each other at top speed for a quarter mile in a straight line—legally or not.

The Pontiac GTO ate up the competition at drag races. A 1964 GTO could chew through a quarter-mile track in 13 seconds. It cruised at 105 miles (169 km) per hour.

Pontiac had hoped to sell 5,000 GTOs in the first year. The company sold 32,000! The car's speed, style, and low price tag made the car very popular.

The Pontiac GTO featured a stock 389-cubic-inch engine with three two-barrel carburetors. Its appetite for speed made it a drag racing champion.

Often considered the pioneer of the muscle car era, the GTO combined a lightweight, mid-size body with a hood scoop and racy trim. The interior featured sporty bucket seats and a floor shifter. John DeLorean, one of the car's designers, insisted on an affordable price tag, too.

THE FASTEST CARS

Muscle car fans often give the GTO credit as the fastest muscle car. Different races—drag or oval track, for example—and various timing methods—acceleration or cruising speed—showed that many different cars blasted out at incredible speeds.

Certainly, other cars had more power than the GTO. Chrysler created many of the high-powered engines. The first North American car to churn up 300 horsepower came from the 1955 Chrysler C300 with a 331-cubic-inch Hemi.

For **street-legal** cars, Chrysler offered the Hemi 426-cubic-inch engine as an option. Chrysler claimed the Hemi design generated 425 horsepower. Drivers insisted it was closer to 500 horsepower. (At the time, many carmakers may have understated their actual horsepower because of insurance costs.)

Chrysler charged $1,100 for the 426 Hemi upgrade. Only about 10,000 cars between 1966 and 1971 rolled out of the factory with the high-performance engine.

What did GTO stand for? Some said, "Gran Turismo Omoligato." Others said, "Grand Touring Option." Insiders at Pontiac said it meant, "Get Those Orders!"

Hemi engines featured rounded—hemispherical—heads instead of flat cylinder heads on the combustion chamber. The cup-like shape boosted the use of heat and space.

The NHRA still sanctions drag races. Today's racers exceed 330 miles (531 km) per hour. They make the stock 1960s muscle cars look pokey.

LEGAL SPEED BATTLES

In the decades before muscle cars reigned, illegal drag races killed and injured countless drivers. Sensing the need for safer racing sites, Wally Parks created the National Hot Rod Association (NHRA) in 1951. His group **sanctioned** the quarter-mile acceleration battles.

Other important organizations formed in the 1960s to sanction races, too. The United States Road Racing Championship (USRRC) held its first professional sports car race at Daytona, Florida, in 1963.

Three years later, the Trans-Am (Trans-American) and Can-Am (Canadian-American) series began with special curved tracks that looked like winding country roads.

Professional Sports Car Racing (PSR), another sanctioning group, started in 1976. Aside from special racing tires and safety equipment, the PSR cars match those available from a dealer. IROC (International Race of Champions) Series also became a popular muscle car competition, frequently dominated by Camaro Z-28s. Today, the National Muscle Car Association hosts races and shows.

RACER CLOSE-UP: CARROLL SHELBY

Carroll Shelby has driven and designed winners for more than fifty years. He started racing cars in 1952. *Sports Illustrated* magazine named him Sports Car Driver of the Year in 1956 and 1957. He quit racing in 1960 when a heart condition side-lined him.

Shelby put his skills to work developing fast cars. The 1960s Shelby Cobras with Ford engines left everyone else in the dust.

In addition to the record-setting cars he built at his Shelby-American factory, Shelby helped build a championship legacy at Ford, Dodge, and Chrysler motor companies. Watch for his new Shelby Series I sports car coming soon!

Handling the furiously fast Shelby Cobra demanded precise skills. Owners took lessons at the Shelby School of High Performance Driving.

CARROLL SHELBY

Born: January 11, 1923

Hometown: Leesburg, Texas

Greatest Victory: Le Mans, 1959

Greatest Car Claim: Shelby Cobra Daytona Coupe won the FIA Federation Internationale de l'Automobile World's Manufacturer's Championship for GT cars on July 5, 1965— the only American car ever

Other Careers: World War II flight instructor and test pilot, dump truck company owner, chicken rancher, Goodyear tire dealer, and founder of The Original Texas Chili Company

The 1970 Shelby GT 350 closed out Ford's "Total Performance" decade.

Ford's 1967 Shelby GT500 with a 428 V-8 could easily hit 0 to 60 in 6.2 seconds or less.

MUSCLE CHAPTER FOUR

Hang On

By 1966, the Ford Shelby Cobra and Chevrolet Corvette both offered stock 427-cubic-inch engines. Anchored in the sleek Corvette, this monster engine could accelerate from 0 to 60 miles (0 to 96.5 km) per hour in less than five seconds and whip past slowpokes at more than 160 miles (257 km) per hour. The Shelby Cobra with the same engine was even faster!

In the 1960s and 1970s, buyers could choose from many different engine sizes, measured in cubic inches or shown as CID (cubic inch displacement).

Even today, more cubic inches mean more horsepower for more speed.

HORSEPOWER HELP

So, what is *horsepower*, anyway?

Way back in the late 1700s, engineer James Watt worked on steam engines. He wanted a way to figure out how much power his engines delivered. Familiar with coal mines, Watt studied the ponies working there. He estimated a pony could lift 550 pounds (885 kg) of coal at a rate of 1 foot (.3 m) per second. He called this unit of power, 550 foot-pounds per second, "horsepower."

Then he converted the timing unit from seconds to minutes. Watt performed more experiments and made his best guess. He judged that horsepower equaled 33,000 foot-pounds of work in one minute.

James Watt figured out horsepower. He is also the man that gave the name "watt" to different sizes of light bulbs, but that's a different story for another book.

Muscle cars engines in the 1960s easily topped 400 horsepower. The Z-28 package on the 1969 Camaro promised a roaring ride!

HOW MUSCLE CARS
LOST HORSEPOWER

Horsepower measurements have not changed since Watt set the standard. But, the way carmakers report horsepower changed in 1972.

Engineers use a **dynamometer** to rate an engine's horsepower. Until 1972, dynamometers tested engines running with just the necessary add-on components—such as fuel, oil, and water pumps. This provided the *gross* horsepower measurement.

The 1972 standard required *net* measurements. This meant testing the engine with *all* of its accessories—including the generator/alternator, starter, emission controls, and exhaust system.

This simple change in reporting hurt the **reputation** of muscle cars. The difference between a gross and net measurement could equal 40 percent. A car with 300 gross horsepower in 1971 suddenly had only 180 net horsepower in 1972. Buyers thought muscle cars had lost their power.

This big block V-8 engine with custom carburetor cover, valve covers, and hose fittings delivers pure power and speed.

In the garage, a special wheeled dolly moves the heavy engine for cleaning, painting, and testing.

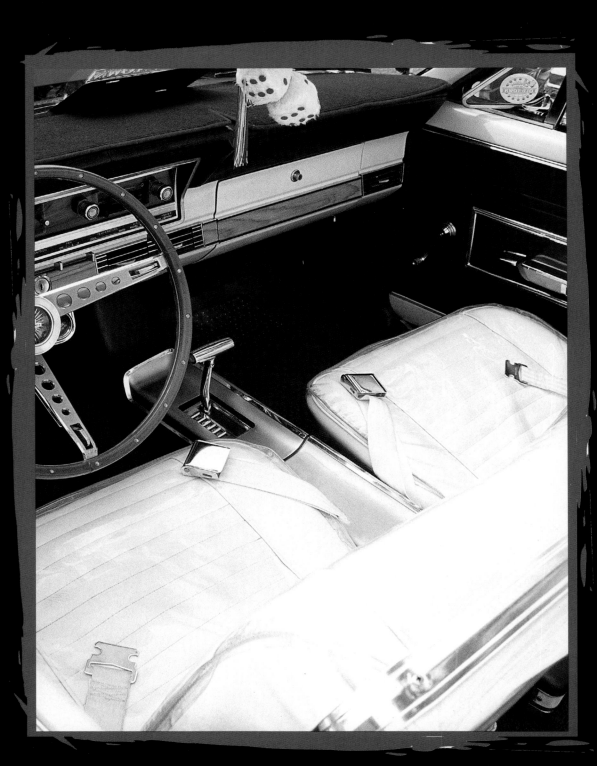

Lap seat belts appeared in some 1960s muscle cars. By the 1970s, shoulder belts became common safety features in all cars.

LATCHING ONTO SAFETY

Muscle cars focused on speed, not safety. Often, engineers designed equipment to add more control for the driver. Wider tires, for example, increased traction. Disc brakes appeared on Mustangs for greater control, too.

Ordinary sedans offered safety belts as an option in the 1950s. Lap belts started to become standard features for 1960s family cars. Mustang racers added seat belts, but most muscle cars did not have them. The more effective shoulder belts finally appeared regularly in cars during the 1970s.

Safety concerns gained momentum then. Ralph Nader's 1965 book *Unsafe at Any Speed* had focused attention on the Chevrolet Corvair. Nader called for more responsible manufacturing practices. The public started to join his safety crusade.

REASONABLE DRIVER SAFETY

Although they never really admitted it, car manufacturers probably knew they had a few dangerous design flaws. Some of their cost-cutting measures proved hazardous, too.

Still, carmakers fought government controls and laws. They argued that reasonable drivers could handle the high-powered cars. True, reasonable people drove muscle cars…but these were reasonable people with a passion for speed. The "bad boy" image of muscle cars grew worse over time as drivers gained a reputation for reckless and deadly driving.

Chevrolet introduced the Camaro after the Corvair became unpopular due to safety concerns.

CHAPTER FIVE

Glory Days

By the first years of the 21st century, "retro" designs and styles appeared everywhere, from toasters in the kitchen to cars on the streets. **Restoration** and **revival** became the two avenues for a return to glory for the muscle car.

RESTORATION PATIENCE

Many of today's muscle car owners now compete for trophies at car shows instead of racing trophies. Car collectors do a lot of work to restore and preserve their vehicles. Joining a car club helps. Members share information, tips, and resources for parts. Most car clubs also keep a list of competitions and shows, as well as the rules for them.

Rescuing a rusted car from the 1960s or 1970s takes time and money. A restoration project, from beast to beauty, can take years of delicate work!

Muscle-car owners might replace a junkyard engine (left) with a powerhouse like this one (right).

(Right)
With time, patience, and money, even this dreary Malibu can look sporty.

(Center and Bottom Right)
Dull gray primer creates a smooth surface and helps the colored paint bond to the metal.

Adding the SS package, new wheels, and other extras creates a new, old car!

PROFESSIONAL CRAFTSMANSHIP

Car owners often pay professionals to handle the difficult painting and **upholstery** restoration work. Toxic painting products require **respirators** and airflow systems. Applying powder coating on parts is tricky, too. The powder dust can ignite!

Many of the winning collector cars feature glamorous finishes, such as see-through pearls, intense candy colors, or shifting **iridescent** tones.

BYPASSING RESTORATION

Restoration remakes an old car into a new, old car. Repli-cars or kit cars allow the owner to build a brand new car with a body style that looks like the original. Several engine manufacturers offer replicated motors, too.

A few buyers completely skip the long restoration process and the complicated repli-car building steps. They buy a ready-to-roll collectible. How much money does it take? A Shelby Cobra, originally $6,000 in 1965, could easily cost $240,000 today—if anyone actually had one for sale!

STAR POWER

Some muscle cars never really disappeared. Just as rock-and-roll bands continued to sing about them, movies and television shows still featured them. Some muscle cars even had names. In the 1980s, the Dodge Charger "General Lee" jumped to fame in *The Dukes of Hazzard* television series. About the same time, "Kit, " a black Pontiac Firebird, "spoke" in the popular *Knight Rider* show.

Muscle cars stole the show in theaters, too. Movies like *Bullet* and *Gone in 60 Seconds* featured classic Mustang action. A Pontiac Trans-Am, with its "screaming chicken" logo on the hood, chased its way to stardom in the 1977 hit *Smokey and the Bandit.* Most recently, the movie *XXX* captured new muscle car fans with its steamy shots of a 1967 Pontiac GTO.

Muscle cars have starred in many hit movies, including The Fast and the Furious *in 2001.*

READY FOR REVIVALS

Ford continues to make Mustangs. Chevrolet still makes Camaros and Corvettes. Recently, Chevrolet revived the Impala. Chrysler brought back the Hemi motor. Even Carroll Shelby has a new "old" model. None possess all the power and glory of the classics, but they're still exciting!

REVVED FOR MORE?

To learn more about muscle cars, take a spin through the local library. Many books and magazines cover these popular vehicles.

Cruise a few museums, such as the Classic Corvettes & Collectibles Museum in Tarpon Springs, Florida, or the Performance Car Museum in Sioux Falls, South Dakota, or one of the many others located across America. The Automobile National Heritage Area in Michigan features nine major automobile sites alone. Detroit is also home to the world's largest car parade. Every year, more than 30,000 amazing vehicles rumble along Woodward Avenue, one of America's best-known cruising roads and a National Scenic Byway.

Several well-maintained Web sites track the shows, cruises, sales, and other events.

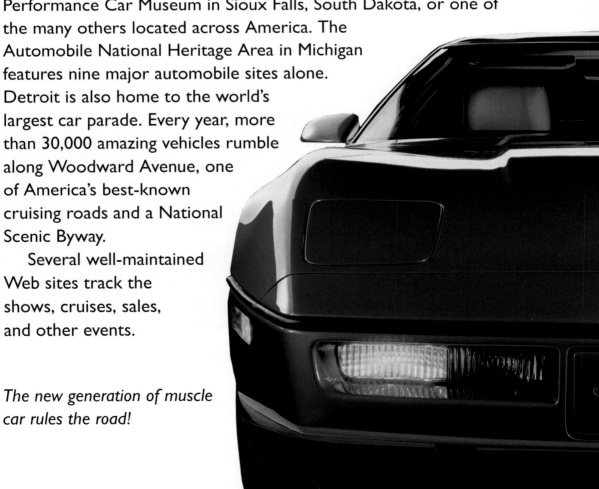

The new generation of muscle car rules the road!

Further Reading

The Encyclopedia of American Muscle Cars by Jim Campisano. Metro Books, 2002.

Great American Muscle Cars: An Imagination Library Series (Cobras, Mustangs, Camaros, Corvettes, Firebirds, GTOs) by Eric Ethan. Gareth Stevens Publishing, 1998.

Mustang Monthly Magazine

Classic Corvettes Museum, Florida

Web Sites

http://www.classiccorvettes.com

http://www.musclecarplanet.com

http://www.cccvette.com/musclecars.htm

http://www.nhra.com/

http://www.carrollshelby.com

http://www.mustangengines.com

http://www.firebirdgallery.com/

http://headsupreview.com/

http://www.NMCA-Racing.com

http://www.noneckschevelle.com

Glossary

acceleration (ak sell ah RAY shun) – the act of increasing speed; pressing the gas pedal to make a car move faster

carburetor (KAR bah ray tur) – a device for mixing fuel with air for the engine to burn

catalytic converter (kat ah LIT ik cahn VUR tur) – a device that helps change toxic pollution from an engine's exhaust into harmless gas and liquid

convertible (kahn VUR tah bull) – a vehicle with a folding top

coupe (KOOP) – a closed, two-door car shorter than a sedan of the same model

dynamometer (dih nah MOM ih tur) – a tool for measuring a vehicle's power

emissions (ih MISH unz) – the pollution and other chemicals released from a car's exhaust

imports (IM ports) – things, such as a vehicle, that are made in another country; a foreign car

iridescent (ir ih DESS ahnt) – lustrous, shimmery, changing colors

louvers (LOO vurz) – a series of narrow openings or slits that allow in air

reputation (rep yah TAY shun) – the opinion other people hold of an individual or group

respirators (RESS pah ray turz) – masks worn over the mouth and nose to protect against harmful air

restoration (ress tah RAY shun) – to return something to its original or normal condition

revival (ri VIY vul) – to bring back; to renew; to make something work again

sanction (SANGK shun) – to approve or to allow; to make rules

sedan (si DAN) – an enclosed automobile body with two or four doors that seats four or more people in two rows of seats

spoiler (SPOY lur) – a fin or blade device that breaks up the air flowing over a car to decrease lift and increase traction at high speeds

stock (STOK) – the standard model or manufacturer's parts of an automobile

street legal (STREET LEE gahl) – a vehicle allowed to be driven on city streets because it meets the standards set by law

upholstery (up HOL stah ree) – in vehicles, the materials, usually fabric or carpet, used to cushion and cover the interior

Index

About The Author

Tracy Nelson Maurer specializes in nonfiction and business writing. Her most recently published children's books include the RadSports series, also from Rourke Publishing LLC. Tracy lives with her husband Mike and two children near Minneapolis, Minnesota.